ADVANCE PRAISE

"Life is made of little and big crossroads, where decisions we make change our world. Some, like leaving a loveless marriage and taking your young children to build another home in a hostile world, are truly weighty and earth-shattering. One strand of lyric poetry has always been about pausing to look over a life—Petrarch, Wordsworth, Bishop, Rich, and Limón have all done this. And so does Pat Owen, not only in this collection but also in her others. Another strand of lyric poetry found in Petrarch and Rich and in Owen is the exploration of love—erotic and familial, obsessive and altruistic, communal and self-love. *The Crossroad* is a journey through memory that examines bold choices, small moments, the recurrent nature of grief, and the many kinds of love that a life might hold, as the poet reckons with the decisions she has made and moves into a new wholeness."

—JEREMY PADEN, author of *World As Sacred Burning Heart*

"Abandoning the life given and taking a chance on happiness, Owen etches an elegy to her beloved—and, by extension, to a host of loved ones—by examining a life well-lived, as if by this one choice, she was destined to cherish every ensuing detail."

—RISA DENENBERG, author of *Rain/Dweller*

"I've been a fan of Pat Owen's spare, perceptive poetry since her first volume, *Crossing the Sky Bridge*, was published in 2016. Now, with her fourth collection, *The Crossroad*, I'm convinced that Owen is a talent deserving of a much wider audience. These poignant and deeply reflective poems capture the essence of life's pivotal moments—from tender memories of family and childhood to profound reflections on grief. '1974 Sanibel Island' chronicles the pain and wonder of choosing your true path, even at the risk of alienating—perhaps even harming—those you love. It beautifully captures a moment in time, blending nostalgia with the tension of impending change.

Sadly, it's followed by a series of poems that chronicle the heartbreaking illness and loss of her beloved. Typical of Owen's poetry, this pain is telegraphed through small moments brilliantly observed. 'Midsummer at its peak now. / Oak leaf hydrangea, / languorous, drooping, lush / with white blossoms. They hang / pendulous as breasts.'

"Always conscious of the sublime in nature, Owen brings a keen eye and a large heart to work that captures the complexity of our interconnected lives with language that's lyrical without being pretentious. Her homage to the poet Marie Howe, titled 'The Gist of the Gist,' might be a description of her own work when she writes, 'I want to see how she / pares away the extraneous / when all we need / is the root dangling with mud / and the blossom glinting / with dew.'"

—PATRICIA AVERBACH
author of *Resurrecting Rain* and *Dreams of Drowning*

"These wry, beautifully observed poems catch and hold the light of a long life well-lived. The opening sequence returns the poet, in memory, to her time as a young mother, when an undeniable new love upended her marriage and changed her life. These are poems of family, community, grief, joy, and tenderness, all infused with an honesty that doesn't shrink from the more difficult moments but renders them in the context of a greater radiance. A profoundly human and moving testimony."
—ALISON LUTERMAN, author of *In the Time of Great Fires* and *Desire Zoo*

"It's January 2025, another crossroad for many Americans to either give in to despair or seek its opposite—hope. Pat Owen's new collection, *The Crossroad*, provides a map for hope, emphasizing the goodness of people, the value of selfless love, the benefits of nature, and the positive experiences that make up a life. How she has found the voice and chosen the details, opening her life to the reader—without becoming sentimental or unrealistic—is remarkable. 'My new neighbor helped me / make Thanksgiving dinner,' she writes, 'the year I was first alone. / It's impossible to forget / such a kindness— / it enters us somehow' ('It Becomes Part of Us'). As Robert Frost suggested, a poem cannot cure the ills of the world, but what it can do is offer 'a momentary stay against confusion.' That stay is what makes Pat Owen's new book valuable."

—Maureen Morehead, Kentucky Poet Laureate 2011–2012

"'I want to know it really happened ('Old Calendars'),' writes Pat Williams Owen in her newest collection, *The Crossroad*, and I hear in this speaker's words a mantra for the way Owen makes her poems. With a documentarian's keen eye and a sojourner's profound attunement to wonder, this poet asks us to look closer at the natural world—'the root dangling with mud / and the blossom glinting / with dew' ('The Gist of the Gist')—and even closer at the human heart."

—Julie Marie Wade
author of *Small Fires*, *When I Was Straight*, and *The Mary Years*

"Loss is the common denominator of the living. How we recover from loss is an individual matter. In her latest collection, Pat Williams Owen charts a journey toward recovery and healing following the death of her beloved, Ellen. Like the well-crafted opening of an engaging novel, story, or film, Owen's title poem provides a glimpse of the end, with only the slightest allusion to all that came before. 'I only knew / I had to leave. I had to choose / a path in tune with my blood / stream. Only then / could I own my bone marrow, / breathe into the depths of my lungs' ('The Crossroad')."

—Deni Naffziger, author of *Strange Bodies*

the CROSSROAD

Also by Pat Williams Owen

Bardo of Becoming
Orion's Belt at the End of the Drive
Crossing the Sky Bridge

PAT WILLIAMS OWEN

the CROSSROAD

POEMS

Shadelandhouse
MODERN PRESS

LEXINGTON, KENTUCKY

A Shadelandhouse Modern Press book
The Crossroad
Poems
Copyright © 2025, Text by Pat Williams Owen
All rights reserved.

For information about permission to reproduce selections from this book, please direct inquiries to permissions@smpbooks.com or to:
Permissions
Shadelandhouse Modern Press, LLC
P.O. Box 910913
Lexington, KY 40591

Published in the United States of America by:
Shadelandhouse Modern Press, LLC
Lexington, Kentucky
smpbooks.com

Printed in the United States of America
First edition 2025
Shadelandhouse, Shadelandhouse Modern Press,
and the logo are trademarks of
Shadelandhouse Modern Press, LLC.

ISBN: 978-1-945049-59-0 (paperback)
ISBN: 978-1-945049-60-6 (epub)

Library of Congress Control Number: 2024952394

Author photo: Jana Glass
Cover and book design: iota books
Cover Art: "Speak to me from everywhere" (oil and wax on wood, 11" x 11") by Laurie Doctor, lauriedoctor.com. Used with the artist's permission.

*In memory of Ellen Bourke Ewing
and for my daughters Kristin and Jennifer*

Contents

one

The Crossroad	1
1974 Sanibel Island	2
Six Thirty Sunday Morning	5
Change the Sheets	6
Midsummer	7
Terry Cloth Robe	8
Three Birds, Hanging Stained Glass	10
Miss You	11
What I Miss	13
August 16 at Cave Hill	14

two

It's This Softness	17
I Try to Remember Her a Toddler	18
Buena Vista, Colorado	19
Warm-Up	21
July 19 Remembered	22
March 11	24
Ode to My Father	25

Hard Church Pews	27
Human Connection	29
In the Waiting Room	30
The Health Department Pool Inspector	31
On the Bridge That Changed Ted Kennedy's Life	33
Centaur	34
Macon, Georgia, Graduation	35

three

After the Death of Thich Nhat Hanh	39
Van Gogh Immersive Experience	40
The Gist of the Gist	41
Marie Howe, the Poet	42
Pádraig Ó Tuama	43
The Sculptor	44
Bookstore Manager	45
A Lesson in Line Breaks	46
Thumbprint	47
Turning on the Impressionistic Mode	48
Construction Site	50

four

Kissing the Mirror	55
Sign at Camp Sanborn	57
HSP	58
Leaving the Party	59
Escaping to the Movies	60
Lunch with Joanne	61
September 1st	62
Old Calendars	63
Wooden Puzzle	64
Dinner at Georgine's	65
Massage Therapist	67
Reacquaintance	68
Forgiveness	69
It Becomes Part of Us	70
Chautauqua Amphitheater Sunday Morning	71
Church of the Palms, Sarasota	73
Before the Service	74
Loretto Motherhouse	75
After So Much Rain	76
Ode to Ibis Always Grazing	77
Sapiens	78

Feral	79
Little Geckos Huddle	80
Returning to Kentucky in Late April	81

Acknowledgments	83
A Note of Gratitude	85
About the Author	87

one

The Crossroad

I used to tell Ellen early on
my heart hurts.
I'd left a sanctioned life,
an approved life.
I'd permanently abandoned
the life I'd been given.
I remember a time sitting
on the floor of the hallway
going through hand-embroidered
linens I'd been given as wedding
gifts and bursting into tears.
I knew I'd hurt and mystified
those close to me.
The effect on my young children
still unknown. I only knew
I had to leave. I had to choose
a path in tune with my blood
stream. Only then
could I own my bone marrow,
breathe into the depths of my lungs.

1974 Sanibel Island

I'm at the pay phone
outside our cottage
nine o'clock every night
the air moist and foggy
the kids finally asleep
and me standing under the glow
of a mellow light
talking to my beloved
three states away.

To get there I drove 1,022 miles,
the captain of this small ship,
kids in the back cheering
the turn of each TripTik page.
It meant we were getting closer to paradise.
What they didn't know—
this wasn't just a vacation.
I see their heads, fragile,
in the rearview mirror.

In memory the three of us walk
the beach searching for shells,
sand buckets in our hands.
My youngest running up to me
holding up a broken sand dollar—
is this one interesting?

After hours collecting shells,
we blow the sand off each one,

wash them in a bucket of water,
place them in careful rows
on the back porch, voting
each day on our favorite.

The pool—a must every afternoon,
kids in inner tubes, twirling
themselves round and round
in circles. Trips to the library,
trips to the craft shop,
sitting on the floor
of the sandy porch playing
Go Fish.

Blond heads, brown shoulders,
the scent of sunscreen,
their long limbs growing so fast.
I'd study them asleep,
trying to envision
an unknown future.
In my mind a magical glow
pervades that time.
Our little world of three.
So much hanging in the balance.

All the while, I ponder
whether I have the grit
to leave a loveless marriage
to be with the woman I love.
I fear losing my children,
as much a part of me

as my blood and bones,
fear the fissure to their world
if I follow my other heart.

All through my child-centered day,
I long for nine o'clock, the receiver
in my hand, speaking with my love
a thousand miles away. The intimacy
of those words spoken under a black,
star-speckled sky. She says she'll drive
down nonstop, an eighteen-hour trip,
to see me after the kids are in bed.

Our love was such,
the sand sparkled,
glittered in the darkness
when we first walked together
on the beach.
I know science can explain this,
but we believed we were magic.

Six Thirty Sunday Morning

We're driving in the dark
to the hospital. The road
eerie quiet, streetlights

shine on wet pavement, only
the squish of the tires breaks
the silence.

A fleeting thought—
this has nothing to do with me.
This is not my journey.

She says *I don't want
to do this test*. I wait for more,
then say *I don't blame you*.

I know my mind is trying
to distance, numb the trauma
of our joint ordeal. Reaching

deep within, I feel around
as though searching a large
cardboard box. I'm looking

for something solid. I slide
my hand from one corner
to the other—

nothing but empty space.

Change the Sheets

Mortality weighs on my shoulders today,
the anniversary of Ellen's death, this day

enshrouded in cool rain. Then there's
Sara's suicide marinating in my cells.

If she can do it, I can do it, demise
just one breath away.

Though I know in my bones,
this is not my path, addicted

as I am to lists and accomplishments.
I can look over the edge of a building

without needing to jump.
I tell myself just do the next things,

simple and grounded as they are,
do my nails, change the sheets.

Midsummer

Midsummer at its peak now.
Oak leaf hydrangea,
languorous, drooping, lush
with white blossoms. They hang
pendulous as breasts.

She could never be happy
till they were trimmed to nubbins.
A sharp blade and broken stems
all over the ground. One year,
in fury at their mutilation,
petulant as a child, I announced
I want to move.
She had destroyed my plants,
killed my desire to be here.

Now, of course, they're back,
heavy with the weight of beauty,
a reminder of my folly,
all that's now gone.

Terry Cloth Robe

I'm still warmed by the terry cloth robe
we bought so many years ago
in Provincetown. I can still see
you donning it on crowded
Commercial Street. Among
a sea of people, you spotted
our friends weaving toward
us and wore it as a joke. In
the parade of outlandishness
(men with plumes in their hats
and parrots on their shoulders),
we were part of the mix.

I hope the robe will still be
here long after I'm gone.
It's now a little worn,
its blue stripes faded, the deep
pockets drooping after years
of toting reading glasses,
fountain pens. Ink stains
permeate the weave.
Made in Turkey
boasts its origins, though
not the origin in my mind.

I envision my daughters
eyeing it, wondering why
I kept it so long. No way
for them to know its meaning:
a grief and consolation
that cannot be moved beyond.
Warmth swaddling
my vulnerable body.

Three Birds, Hanging Stained Glass

The sun has to be low on the horizon
and then the birds catch fire, glow.
What was before unremarkable
now shines, pulses with an inner blaze.
The one on the far right has a red eye,
the one in the middle sparkles like glitter.
They all shine like sunlight on water,
a warm golden shimmer.

Like an ordinary Thursday afternoon
unloading groceries from the car and then
remembering love
that moment of brilliant light.

Miss You

Wish you could come back
for maybe just a day. We
could hang out. I could tell you
what's happened since you've
been gone. Little Claire
is now a grown-up ballerina,
from her childhood after-dinner show
to a real-world lighted stage. Barrett,
still a stunning beauty, is working
on sustainability under
Colorado big skies.

I miss you tucking me in, stopping
whatever you were doing to say
goodnight, kiss me. Remember
how you always wanted me
to come into the bedroom with you
while you changed your clothes
after work? We'd talk about
our days. I miss that.

You always said we were the same
age though we weren't. A unified
front. Now I use our initials and
birthdates as my password. You've
been gone so long you don't know
what that means but I'll catch you
up. Bright as a shooting star. You'll
catch on quick.

You can tell me about where you are now. For so long I chanted *why did you leave me?* And still, I calculate time from before and after you left.

What I Miss

The absolute goodness in my life,
someone who always had my best interest
in mind. I thought I could find this again,
that it would be drawn to me like a magnet.
Turns out I was wrong, assuming goodness
when it was a flimsy apparition.

What I miss is your gift of laughter, turning
even a cancer diagnosis into a lighthearted
view, singing I left my breast at MD Anderson
and calling me Nurse Fuzzy Wuzzy as I changed
your bandage.

In Granada, you left the tour group to buy
a journal you knew I'd treasure. In Bloomington,
you ran down the street to buy a poem from
a street poet. You memorized all the places
I lived as a child and recited them as though
a sacred text. If I hit my crazy bone, you'd
say I'm sorry that happened to you.

I miss our common assumption about
how we'd live, good food as a matter
of course, gifts of the highest quality,
expertly wrapped. I miss your fierce
love that would go to any length to protect
me, make me happy. This love so fierce
it survived death, surrounds me
even now.

August 16 at Cave Hill

Dear Baby,

Early this morning in the dark,
a light flickered high on the wall
above my bed. In this world
of mysteries it was probably
a reflection but I wondered
if it was you. Are the dead
aware of the living? Everything
in me wants to say yes.

The ground here is dry
and parched and I don't
understand anything
more than I ever did.
Sometimes I think you'll
just appear, I'll walk
in the house and there
you'll be, or I'll drive
in our old neighborhood
and you'll be walking Saxon.
Who knows what happened
to the past? A few drops
of rain and I head to the car
with you, without you.

two

It's This Softness

Now that I'm tender enough, strong enough,
aware enough to open up, it's almost time

to go and instead of turmoil
what I really want is to sit on the porch watching

the sparse leaves caressed by the breeze.
It's this softness I was meant for,

not stomach-clenching conflict. I don't want
to be defended but sturdy and strong.

Visions of my father walking down Fourth Street,
erect carriage, head high.

I Try to Remember Her a Toddler

standing in front of the fridge,
watermelon juice streaked down
her chest. She was all mine,
recently part of my body.
I could sweep her up, face
to face, kisses all over her head.
You are my sweet baby I'd chant,
putting her in a basket on my bike,
peddling around the neighborhood
describing all we were seeing.

Now I go to her for advice, she
solid and professional in her
long white lab coat, a responsible
mother with adult daughters
of her own.

I try to bring back holding her close
in a waiting room
her small body hot, fast-beating heart,
temple wet against my own,
stroking her head, tender
and soft as a melon. Every ounce
of my will lasered to keeping
her alive. Our survival interlocked.

Buena Vista, Colorado

My grandkids are out running in this eight-thousand–
foot altitude, rugged and fearless, faces
alight. The atmosphere is rarified,
the air crystalline, the clothes formfitting,
lightweight, insulated, and waterproof.
This stuff could go to the moon.

And today I'm going with them
despite the flab on my belly
and my many decades on earth.
They kindly stop to rest with me
several times on our loop, with not
a shred of disparagement.

We're surrounded by saturated
blues and greens, the tawny tan
of sandstone. Striding head of me
on the path, my granddaughters
almost identical,
their broad shoulders
and long-legged loose gait,
blond hair swinging, glinting
in the sun. These young
Amazons thrived in a time
when their strength was affirmed.
As I huff and puff, I imagine
my wind at their backs.

Mountain bikers careen by us
through the narrow rocky-ridged
path, down below fly fishermen
in waders and the laughter of kids
in inflated river rafts. Exuberance
sparkles in the air. We breathe
it all in.

Warm-Up

They're bouncing like puppies
these cross-country runners
adolescents still growing
into their long limbs
and Adam's apples.
Like pogo sticks up and down
one straight leg stretched high
and then the other.
They're prancing before the run,
a spectacle to convince their opponents
and themselves
they're fierce, invincible.
And then they form a team circle
arms around each sweaty shoulder,
heads together,
a chant, and then a scream
from the bottom of each lung
and like all the warriors before them
they charge onto the field.

July 19 Remembered

I can't imagine it wasn't sweltering
on this midsummer day, ninety years
ago when my parents married, she
a schoolgirl of sixteen, he an aspiring
pastor. Rural, unsophisticated,
they had chosen each other.
With both families standing
in witness, they were joined
in matrimony by a local preacher.

No honeymoon, she moved
into his family home presided
over by his mother. Many
listening ears that night.
In a crowded household,
how far away could they get?

Even now, I'm haunted
by how profoundly
their lives were changed
that day. Steadfast
in their devotion
for over fifty years. Daily,
he tried to please her.
Caretaking to the end,
she assured he wore
matching socks
in his coffin.

Now, as then, tall trees
sway, the sky a muted
blue, softened with clouds,
and I, their firstborn,
still contemplate that day.
Was I there in some form?
A consciousness in
waiting?

March 11

When the calendar nears
Daddy's birthday
I'm conscious of it
as though moving toward radium
which puts off light,
glows of itself.

I find words in my handwriting
at the top of my notebook
After death we'll be consciousness
in another form.

Ode to My Father
After Denise Duhamel

Man of making breakfast for the kids
French toast slightly charred
with sweet maple syrup.

Man of newspaper reading late afternoon
feet on the ottoman, standing lamp glowing.
He of soft hands, books stacked nearby.

Man with errands to run, cleaners and car wash,
helping around the house with laundry, vacuuming.
He called someone else to make repairs.

Man of hands upraised in the pulpit, inviting forward
those who yearned to be saved, visiting parishioners
in the hospital, holding their hands in his.

He of Sunday afternoon lemonade and hand-cranked
peach ice cream, crushed ice and salt overflowing,
man of a sweet tooth who would eat sugar on a biscuit.

Man of dress clothes—shirt with a collar and dress pants,
no T-shirt and jeans, man of ironed boxer shorts
who drank his instant coffee from a Melmac cup.

Sports-loving man, watching wrestling on a Sunday afternoon
until he decided to boycott because of beer ads,
man who listened to boxing matches on the radio.

Sponsor of family picnics in the park, a wicker basket
of fried chicken and potato salad, slick red plastic plates,
man of taking the kids to the doctor, school conferences.

Minister proud of his funerals, dignity and honor freely bestowed
a scholar of hymns, ritual, prayers,
a hand around a shoulder, words of comfort.

He of the twenty-minute power nap
man of family board games, head-back belly laugh,
shiny black Bible smooth to the palm.

Man of hands with no calluses,
made as they were for turning pages,
making outlines, soothing the distressed—
man of walking with shoulders back,
head high
and I his resilient daughter.

Hard Church Pews

Even now after all these years
I remember my made-up
sign language. I can recite it
in my head and still make the shapes
with my hands. It helped me survive
endless church services, Sunday
morning, Sunday night, Wednesday night.
Complaints would have done
no good. Church was an unquestioned
part of my life like brushing my teeth
and going to school. It's what we did.

Then there were the undercover games
with the hymnals, a sort of scavenger hunt:
go to page 78 and then to page 32, etc.,
and ultimately some payoff with what
we thought was funny.
    Do you have Prince Philip in a can?
    Let him out.

Hours of gazing at the backs of heads,
faces in the choir, making up stories
about them as though they were characters.
Strangely, I never read a book there, probably
not allowed, though I read everywhere else.
Remembering the arms of boys around
me at the movies, fantasies occupied
my mind while my body sat on hard pews.

On the bulletins, we scribbled arrows,
boxes, simple designs, anything to make
time pass, leave our mark.

Human Connection

The service manager from Sam's Auto Care
picks me up in his wide Ram truck.
Once a week he hand-polishes the chassis,
and it glows, new and shiny red.

He tells me his kids visit on the weekend
and his seventeen-year-old now lives with him.
That's the way of the world I say.
Lines crinkle around his eyes, he nods,
acknowledges our hard-earned
expertise on kids.

I tell him even though it cost too much
I ordered a new service manual
for my car since the old one was falling
apart. He says it's important to preserve
what we have. We ride in silence,
in our common understanding.

In the Waiting Room

The Black man sits before me
praying to his phone
long thin legs
stretch out before him.
His hiking boots
have orange laces.
He's immaculate
in crisp navy shorts
and soft lavender hoodie.
He's studious, contained,
a scholar, I suspect.
I can't quite make out
the title of the book on his lap.
I'd like to strike up a conversation
but don't know how.
In my mind I fantasize
I like your boots, where
do you hike? what
are you reading? wanna
get some lunch when we finish
up here? I could imagine
driving cross-country
with him so we'd have space
to talk, explore every idea
that comes up. Even though
I say nothing, in another
lifetime, I could love him.

The Health Department Pool Inspector

takes his position seriously.
With his authority to shut
down the pool
for any small infraction,
he takes his time making the rounds,
especially if condo residents
are present. In his cargo shorts
and navy polo shirt, he strides
around the pool, with military
efficiency, speaking briskly to each
swimmer and lounger
in turn. Good morning, how
are you today? I feel like
we should click our heels and salute.

Then over the next twenty minutes,
he scrutinizes the chemicals with care,
rechecks them, examines
the lock on the gate, studies
the emergency phone, ascertains
there aren't too many people
in the pool, inspects the condition
of the rescue equipment and the contents
of the skimmer baskets.

Then he pores over his cell phone
and his clipboard notepad
one more time, makes the rounds
again, just to be sure. Finally,
with a great flourish,
Ladies, I bid you good day.

Me to my friend, I'm surprised
I didn't get cited for my feet
on the table. And she to me,
Yea, that blue nail polish—
I'm sure that's not regulation.

On the Bridge That Changed Ted Kennedy's Life

the bridge with no guardrails,
we chose between small twigs
to play Poohsticks:
whose stick would float fastest in the current
from one side of the bridge to the other.
We played a child's game on the bridge
that should have been named
The Mary Jo Kopechne Memorial Bridge
but money won out
and fifty years later
no sign marks the spot
and only old-timers know
the almost-forgotten story
how death and escape
and scandal and cover-up
happened here.

Centaur

With the tall, long-boned
frame of a basketball player

his large hands could cradle
the rough orange orb and spring

to score a three-point shot.
His narrow long face

and big teeth, equine
and masculine, highlight

an aw-shucks charm. He's self-
effacing with a big smile and a mane

of hair falling loose. He always
has something to say, often

a contrarian, male
point of view. The heart

of his being merges man
with just a hint of beast.

I admire from a distance
but on safari
I'd never get too close—
never take my foot off
the gas pedal of the Jeep.

Macon, Georgia, Graduation

In bright formals and tuxes
with red cummerbunds,
the graduates one by one
dutifully climb
into a horse-drawn carriage
and are driven around a circle
in the hotel parking lot
by a Black driver,
cigarette dangling from his lips.
He's watched all these kids
and their parents grow up.
Stoicism embedded
in the lines around his eyes.

Once around the lot
and out they go
with others waiting their turn
just like in kindergarten
with pony rides,
when Mama with camera
waited nearby. Then,
as now, they're props
in an ancient ritual.

three

After the Death of Thich Nhat Hanh

In the shining meditation hall
floors polished to a high gloss
mellow sounding of the bell.
Brown-robed monks
in straight rows
lined up like soldiers
heads shaved bare as knobs
chanting in unison.

Clarity and space in the hall.
I know just what it feels like
to be there though we watch
on a screen.

My mind goes to figuring out
which monks are men
and which are women.
The women slighter,
the men with a shadow
of a beard, protruding
Adam's apple.

Then I watch my mind
wondering what drew
the monks to this spartan life—
a life apart, a different
way to be. The hall echoes—
vibrates
with the sound of the bell.

Van Gogh Immersive Experience

Spills of color flow across the walls
and floor, covering even the observers
who become part of the art. We're
all one in this world. Classical music
embraces us. It's like a drug trip
without the drugs.

The multitude of faces he painted, haunted
in their tenderness, eyes ranging
from dull to agonized to stunned.

How does this perfectly ordinary
kid pictured in the entry become
the genius brightening the world?
How does he avoid being drowned
by the mundane and instead shine
a light on all our lives?

His many self-portraits ask the question,
who am I? The anguish of the cut-off ear.

After being drenched in all this color,
like Easter eggs dipped in dye
we emerge a shade different
than when we entered.

The Gist of the Gist

All Marie Howe tries to do:
communicate the essence
of being alive.
And she does it sparingly,
with no unnecessary words—
just the gist of the gist.
I want to see how she
pares away the extraneous
when all we need
is the root dangling with mud
and the blossom glinting
with dew.

Marie Howe, the Poet

Marie Howe is always chewing on her lips,
the top one full as though plumped
with snuff.

She chews on them highlighting
their sensuality as though she can't
quite let them go, they're too delicious.

Her wild hair falls round her shoulders
like a waterfall. She pushes it away
from her eyes with the back of her hand.

Her poems, poignant as a heartbeat,
root out the marrow of any bone.

Pádraig Ó Tuama

No wonder his body suffered
a decade-long autoimmune disease,
his body attacking itself, joining
the assaults of the world.

I know something of this pain,
growing up in a strict religious
environment and abandoning
that community and teachings.

An outcast for so long,
he grew from a place of torment
and out of that wringer emerged
a seasoned wisdom.

Now he speaks with the tenderness
with which you'd greet a newborn.
The crinkly smile lines around
his eyes have seen it all.

The Sculptor

She floats just slightly off the ground,
ignores emails but thinks
she's answered them, lives
in a neverland breathing a potion
rarer than oxygen, more refined,
an elixir of the gods. She even
dreams in epic terms—white lions
by her side, her guardians
and coat of arms.

Her smile radiates, lights an aura
around her. Her shape
conjures an ancient fertility
goddess someone pulled out
of a tomb, blew the dust from.

I imagine her, strong arms
deep in clay,
hands molding new life,
forming what has never
been before.

I, a mere mortal,
nightly pray
for such dreams, such magic.

Bookstore Manager

James wears a dark T-shirt,
and, with a long-woven scarf
tied around his neck, he looks
like a Frenchman, head shaved,
a heavy beard neatly sheared.
I imagine the harsh beginning
each day of a soaped scraped
neck. And though his skin
is festooned with tattoos,
he looks scrubbed clean
from the shower. Mala beads
encircle his wrist and speak
of a deep well to draw from.
He would fit in an Italian
Renaissance painting done
in dark heavy oils, and around
him rich warm colors glow
with light.

A Lesson in Line Breaks

Dear Stephanie,
I can see from your lack
of response
you're not interested
in communicating
with me.
From you,
I learned much
about line breaks,
trusting the image,
showing not telling.
Many of your students
continue to benefit
from your support.
However,
not me.
It's clear I don't mirror
your worldview,
I'm not molded in your image,
didn't grow up abused
on the streets of the ghetto.
You owe me nothing
of course,
and I tell myself
I can let go
of disappointment.

Thumbprint

Today my new book will arrive,
in a big cardboard box, the books
green-covered and filled with my life.
I'm anticipating this event like a woman
with a belly long swollen in Houston in August.
How long I've awaited this day—
nine months at least, an appropriate
time for the birth of a child. Though the poems
took years to create.

My baby's almost here and what will I do
with her, yearning to be worthy of this life,
my DNA in print. There's nothing
like seeing it in final form, in the flesh
so to speak, to hold it, to know
it's real, a tangible being to leave behind
with my distinctive thumbprint.

Turning on the Impressionist Mode

My new tree, the Shady Lady,
still young, a kid of a tree,
now draped in Spanish moss,
gray beards of sorrow
enough to weigh down
a young spirit. And
now a torrent of rain
out of nowhere. My phone
says it isn't happening
but out my open window
I see it peppering
the canal. The clean
smell of rain wafting in—
breeze cool and damp
on my skin. Golf carts
evaporated from the expanse
of green. And now
the rain has disappeared
as quickly as it started.
Is it safe to venture out
for my walk? A cloud-
mottled sky, strips of blue
behind the clouds, a general
brightening. I think I'll risk
it, rain jacket tied around
my waist. I'm listening
intently for what comes next.

Carlton gone, Barbara gone,
figures in my mind no longer
here on this plane. Heron
tiptoes by, deliberate
on thin pipe-cleaner legs.

Construction Site

I've watched the fitness center grow
day by day, straight walls
ascending block by block,
mudded into place, an easy swipe
with a trowel, dark grainy wetness
smeared smooth. As the roof
takes shape, men balance
on raw wood beams, catch two-by-fours
tossed to them from the ground.

The men, maybe one woman,
wear hard hats and on each worker
faded jeans and brown, laced boots,
the outline of a phone in a back pocket.

Every day as I walk by, I count them,
I can't tell you why,
usually seven to ten workers
including the guy in the backhoe.
They don't work on the weekend
and when I walk by then, I hope
they're resting, enjoying their families.

The most heart-stopping part,
when a guy balancing on a wall
is catching a beam being lowered
to him from a tall crane,
an act worthy of Wallenda. I pause,
holding my breath, and gasp when
it's firmly in his hands.

But my favorite part of the construction
site, the resident dog, a mongrel,
black and white, mostly Australian
shepherd, who follows at the heels
of the site manager as he talks to clumps
of workers, checks his phone and clipboard,
goes to the porta-potty. The dog waits
patiently outside, a scene straight out
of Norman Rockwell. Why does this
make me so happy? It feels like
a community and as I walk by,
I'm somehow part of it.

four

Kissing the Mirror

I remember
alone in the bathroom
practicing kissing the mirror
making it soft, sensuous, delicious.
Tentative, my tongue wet
against the cool glass.

My sex education,
self-directed,
came from reading
every forbidden book I could find
and from the *Marriage Counseling Manual*
on my father's office shelf.
I'd sit on the floor
devouring every page,
though the words
were unpronounceable.
In my head *penis*
reads *pen* (like ink pen) *us*.

In church,
my father, high above
in the pulpit,
looks down on me in the fourth row,
pink cheeked, freshly scrubbed.

Though my body submits
to hard pews,
my mind drifts
to Saturday matinees,
a boy's arm around my shoulder
and warmth percolating my core.

I'm beginning to see through a new lens.

I allow myself
an inner benediction,
inner shooting stars.

Sign at Camp Sanborn

A shark in an aquarium will grow 8 inches,
a shark in the ocean will grow 8 feet.
The same is true of you.

What if I hadn't been such a rule
follower? Would I be enlarged
by adventures? More oxygen
in my blood, quicker firing synapses?
More alive, days not blurring
one into another?

Would I have sheltered in a foreign
land, my shoulders broader,
taking on the persona of the heroic,
my chest bursting the seams
of my Superwoman outfit?

Of course, behind this drama
hangs the curtain of Karma.
We all arrive with defined parents,
genes, protoplasm.

It's not nothing.

At the end of the day, I'd like to say
I've chosen. I grew here,
as tall as I could. And
I've left these words.

HSP

This is me,
my new letters—
just found out
it has a name:
Highly Sensitive Person.
It's a relief to know
I'm not alone, it's
a nervous system thing,
not a choice.
Some psychologists
identified this—
wrote a book.
Who knew?
It means I'm easily overwhelmed, depleted,
overly affected by loud noises, bright lights,
highly attuned to stimuli.
I remember times where everyone
else was happy staying late singing
Christmas carols and I longed to be home
snuggled in bed. Or the time I left
the Tina Turner concert early, not because
I didn't admire her talent and legs that
went on forever, her mortal-defying energy,
but because the flashing strobes and crushing
sound made my heart pound in my ears.

The only problem with this designation
it's like saying to people
you'll have to pardon me—
I'm a diva.

Leaving the Party

I know I must weave my way
through the clinking of glasses,
through the crowd, voices raised
to be heard over the music,
past the server with trays
of champagne, to thank
my host, which means
interrupting her conversation,
then approach the honored
guest, waiting until the eyes
of the huddled threesome
turn to me, say goodbye to her,
wade through more people
juggling drinks and small plates,
past the waiter with a silver tray
of elegant bruschetta, past
groups of three or four huddled
together laughing, find other
close friends to say goodbye,
try to explain without insult
I'd rather just be home
alone.

Escaping to the Movies

I love going to the movies alone
in the middle of the day—
something illicit about it
like having an affair
without the guilt.
You're a kid playing hooky.
Get lost in the larger-
than-life screen,
Technicolor far brighter
than the drab outside.
Go ahead and get popcorn
and a Coke, both your
mouth and heart satiated.
Instant gratification,
all the salt and crunch
and sparkly sugar
your cells can absorb.

Lunch with Joanne

She approaches my umbrella picnic
table with a warm smile, an assured
step, radiating clarity and kindness.

Bald head just sprouting new growth,
hard to disguise that pallid after-chemo
look but she says amazing how her body
came through it, gratitude in her DNA.

She comes with her handsewn cloth bag
with her cloth napkin, apple, and hard-
boiled egg. Like her lunch, she's modest,
unassuming, neutral cotton top and flared
Indian pants. Our conversation is quiet.
I tell her I know more about chemo
than I care to. We're tender with each other.
We know softness, we know strength
when we see it.

September 1st

It always gets to be September 1st
ready or not
and it's not as though
you haven't noticed time passing
how Wednesdays turn into Thursdays
and then Fridays
and suddenly the morning
is darker and cooler
an abrupt reminder
of time passing
and you're thinking of packing up
and heading south
but first the nod to transition
still ancient in the bones
back to school
the thought of sliding
into a denim shirt and jeans
so soft on the skin.

Some part of us dreads the change,
we don't want to proceed
into the darkness ahead
with the long warm days
by the pool still fresh in our minds.
We've watched this wheel turn
so many times before.
We can do it again.
We know we can.

Old Calendars

I've wondered why I've kept
all these stacks of slick Sierra Club
spiral-bound desk calendars
filled with shiny nature pictures
and my inked notes
of all my activities for years—
a stack a foot high on a shelf
in my bedroom. Tennis dates,
dinner plans, book groups, vacations.
Of what possible use other
than history? All I can tell you
is I want to remember time
because it slides so inexorably away.
I want to know it really happened.

Wooden Puzzle

What is it my fingers seek?
The intricate fitting
together of pieces, the click
of lock and groove,
the long, silent
attention required
to see gradations
of color, pattern.
Or maybe it's the quiet
access to the unconscious
where we dwell
in watchful waiting.

Dinner at Georgine's

It's all going to be carryout
and that's fine with me.
We share the view
there are things we'd rather do
than cook.

Her living room is a cocoon—
a library retreat of sorts.
Drapes drawn, a cozy-lit
warmth, stacks of books
on every table and shelf.
She turns off the music
so we can have our silence,
just the two of us
bouncing ideas off one another,
what we think,
what we feel, what
we judge important.
My faith perhaps more metaphoric
than hers, but still we connect.

I sit on a genuine leather couch.
On the dark walls, oil paintings
she brought back from Turkey.
Live plants surround us.
Nothing here is fake.

We share stories
we might not tell anyone else,

stories of transcendence,
pillars of light, transfigured
faces. Georgine, an Episcopal
priest, believes she does
the Lord's work, and I
can't disagree. Her years
as nursing home chaplain
and counselor to clergy
in distress make her an expert
in life's catastrophes.

She meets everyone
with warmth and acceptance
and maybe that's all
any of us need.

Massage Therapist

She told me
all the many ways
her mother
had tried to abort her.
Through all her growing up,
had called her
lard butt and
dumb bunny.

But now years later
she brings her tall thin
frame to the massage table
and gives herself over
to my body there,
anointed with oil,
enveloped in tenderness,
caressed like a newborn.

In her focused meditative state
I become the beloved
child, the one for whom
she's responsible, whose
happiness depends on her.

Reacquaintance

She's just moved into my neighborhood
and I hope we can become friends.
I remember her fondly from tennis.
I liked her open, honest face,
her forthright demeanor. She
relates how intimidating it was
to join our tennis group, brings
up my net game, wants to know
why I no longer play.

When I tell her my age,
she gasps,
lowers her head toward the table.
A pause before she can speak,
a slight shake of her head.
Wow, you're in good shape.
It was almost as though
I had revealed myself
as another species
or as though
I were cracked,
an almost hidden fissure
through the core of my being.
Will we be able to be friends
still, or am I now only fit
for the remaindered bargain table
at the bookstore?

Forgiveness

For staying only forty minutes
at the neighborhood pizza party,
I forgive myself. Also, for not
saying goodbye

to the woman sitting next to me,
the need to leave more pressing
than niceties though the leaving
causes her to call asking

if I'm ok. Anyway, I forgive
my inability to linger over small talk
when the more-compelling
Amazon Prime series awaits.

I forgive my need for quiet
and solitude, a need as deep
as breathing. I have mercy
on my desire for space

to see the world on my own terms.
I forgive my lack of perfection,
never as smart or kind as I'd like.
Only gazing at high-flying birds

brings peace and only
deep breath, ease.

It Becomes Part of Us

My new neighbor helped me
make Thanksgiving dinner
the year I was first alone.

It's impossible to forget
such a kindness—
it enters us somehow,
becomes one with the bloodstream,
breathes with us,
in and out,

absorbs into the lining
of the lungs, attaches to our blood
cells, flows through the scarlet-lined
arteries into the tingling capillaries,
pumped by the beating red
of the heart.

Chautauqua Amphitheater Sunday Morning

The blue-robed choir never stops
their fervent singing
though medics are rushing down the steps
to assist the man crumpled
to the floor. They kneel around him,
like attending angels,
with one tech lifting a glucose bag
toward the sky.

His wife in a crisp striped shirt
stands frantically tapping
on her cell phone. Nearby,
people are passing cushions
to prop up his body.
It feels like sirens should be screaming.
I'm holding my breath. My stomach
a gripped fist. Why is it taking
so long? Someone hugs
the wife. The organ,
triumphant, plays on.

I keep checking my watch.
Millennia pass. Finally,
four medics carry him
in a blue rubber sling
up the steps. Behind them

the woeful parade of wife,
family, and friends.
The choir continues to sing.

My mind remains on the fallen
man even after the fiery woman
priest, collared and Episcopal,
begins her sermon. Still,
I can't concentrate. When
have our own cries been unheard?

How quickly we can crumple,
hoping kind hands will be there
to lift us up.

Church of the Palms, Sarasota

This Twenty-First–Century Church
believes in meeting people
where they are.

I found nirvana on the air-conditioned
pickleball courts along with a woman
playing with a portable oxygen tank
and a finger oxygen meter. Same church
where I saw a comfort dog in a stroller
wheeled into Sunday morning worship.
You can choose a Sunday School class
on "Creating with Color," or take
a Zoom class with the minister
on the work of C.S. Lewis, or join
a book group where you're divided
into groups of six in separate rooms
for better discussions. There are options
for Zumba, yoga, volleyball, grief counseling,
couples counseling, and tango lessons.

Before the Service

The vaulted ceiling filled
with crystalline light,
music bright in the air
brilliant as heaven.
I sit in church visualizing
my final day unfolding there.
I imagine my grandchildren
sitting in a row
clean and glowing
with young health.
The familiar words
of ritual come back.
I am the resurrection
and the life, whosoever
believes in me shall never die.
My spirit now as clear
as human flesh can be.
It's a place of enchantment
where I'm as innocent,
forgiven as a child.

Loretto Motherhouse

I love that you can't buy
anything here.
Everything simple, clean,
homespun: hand-needled
footstools, quilts draped
over chairbacks. Wood floors
shine with caretaking.

During the night,
the clanging of radiators
waking up, a *shing*
of steam heat.

Like being on safari
in the bush, here
we're returned
to the natural world.
I'm resting on a bench
watching leaves wave
against a blue sky.

After So Much Rain

Last night in my headlights
frogs no bigger than matchbooks
bounced in high arcs
two and three feet high
across the wet road
just ahead of my squishing tires.

Ode to Ibis Always Grazing

You forever speck the green mounds
of wet grass,
head down,
you graze.
With orange legs
and curved beak,
your timeless form belongs
in ancient Egypt,
but here you are in my backyard—
the common chicken
of the golf course.

Sapiens

As I drive across town alone,
it's not just me in the car
but also floating in my bloodstream
memories of the African savannah,
my peripheral vision keen to any movement
and riding along with me,
the long-honed instincts
of the mountain gorilla
and the narrowed eye of the hawk.

Some part of me is always
on alert for danger
and warns me with breezes
coming in through the gill slits—
a slight rise of hair on my arms,
saliva pooling in the back
of my throat.

Feral

Something in this word
speaks to my DNA. It's where
we came from when we lived
in the trees, the caves. I sense
it in my night vision,
eyes narrowed
making out shapes in the shadows,
alert to movement,
any sign of threat.

Every challenge to us
is like a pencil sharpening,
a weapon honed,
we stay awake—
alert to the next coiled snake.

Little Geckos Huddle

inside the screens of my sliders.
Who can blame them? It's
raining out and will be all day.
They breathe in the dampness
and feel the drops blow in
on their soft green bodies.

We all do the same—
seek protection from whatever's
out there—danger, discomfort.
We've got our raincoats,
our seat belts, our insurance
policies. Creatures
seeking shelter.

Still, we all know
from the last hurricane,
our efforts may be a white flag
blowing in the wind.

Returning to Kentucky in Late April

The weather raw and damp,
gray sky, the trees a spring green,
aching in newness.
Ghosts at each intersection I pass.
Losses I can put behind me
while far away spring at me now
like cat's teeth at my neck.

I could be in the tropics
under blue skies and a bright sun,
but I chose to be here, though
I'm ambushed at every turn.

Do I only imagine tears swelling
my throat? A sadness that would
drain me dry if I'd let it. But of course,
I won't, practiced as I am
in turning away.

Acknowledgments

My thanks to the editors of the following publications in which these poems in the collection have previously appeared, sometimes in an earlier form:

Atlanta Review
"1974 Sanibel Island"

The Hong Kong Review
"The Crossroad"
"Midsummer"
"Returning to Kentucky in Late April"

Highland Park Poetry
"Sapiens"

The Louisville Review
"I Try to Remember Her a Toddler"

Raven's Perch
"It Becomes Part of Us"

A Note of Gratitude

Many thanks to my Bookstore1Sarasota Poetry Group: Georgia Court, Linda Robiner, Don McLagan, Pat Averbach, Susan Nusbaum, and Bubba Henson. Also, to my Spalding Poetry Group: Lennie Hay, Anne Bucey, Lynette Lamp, Quincy McMichael, and Carol Grossman. Thanks to Deni Naffziger for helpful comments on the manuscript and to Alison Luterman for her ongoing support of my work.

About the Author

PAT WILLIAMS OWEN is the author of four poetry books, including *The Crossroad* (Shadelandhouse Modern Press, 2025), *Bardo of Becoming* (Accents Publishing, 2022), *Orion's Belt at the End of the Drive* (Accents Publishing, 2019), and *Crossing the Sky Bridge* (Larkspur Press, 2016). Her work has appeared in *Gulf Stream Magazine, Highland Park Poetry, The Hong Kong Review, The Louisville Review, Raven's Perch*, other print and online literary journals, and several anthologies. She was a finalist in the Atlanta Review International Poetry Competition and an award winner in the Chautauqua Writers' Center 2020 Literary Arts Contest.

www.ingramcontent.com/pod-product-compliance
Lightning Source LLC
Chambersburg PA
CBHW060535080526
44586CB00012B/741